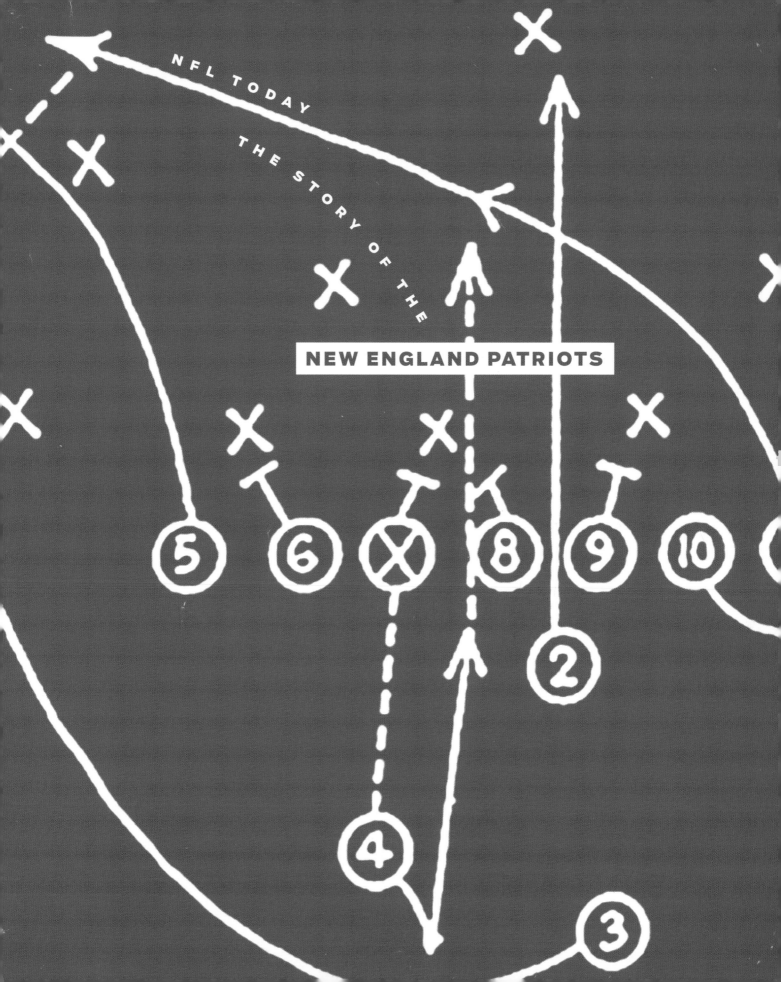

THE STORY OF THE NEW ENGLAND PATRIOTS

JIM WHITING

CREATIVE EDUCATION

PUBLISHED BY CREATIVE EDUCATION
P.O. BOX 227, MANKATO, MINNESOTA 56002
CREATIVE EDUCATION IS AN IMPRINT OF THE CREATIVE COMPANY
WWW.THECREATIVECOMPANY.US

DESIGN AND PRODUCTION BY BLUE DESIGN
ART DIRECTION BY RITA MARSHALL
PRINTED IN THE UNITED STATES OF AMERICA

PHOTOGRAPHS BY CORBIS (BETTMANN), GETTY
IMAGES (ARTHUR ANDERSON/NFL, DOMINIC CHAVEZ/
BOSTON GLOBE, BARRY CHIN/BOSTON GLOBE,
TIMOTHY A. CLARY/AFP, SCOTT CUNNINGHAM,
JONATHAN DANIEL/ALLSPORT, JIM DAVIS/BOSTON
GLOBE, DAVID DRAPKIN, STEVE DUNWELL, GIN ELLIS/
NFL PHOTOS, ELSA, FOCUS ON SPORT, JEFF HAYNES/
AFP, WALTER IOOSS JR./SPORTS ILLUSTRATED, NICK
LAHAM, STREETER LECKA, NEIL LEIFER/SPORTS
ILLUSTRATED, ANDY LYONS, JIM MCISAAC, DONALD
MIRALLE, RONALD C. MODRA/SPORTS IMAGERY, NFL,
DARRYL NORENBERG/NFL, DOUG PENSINGER, HY
PESKIN/SPORTS ILLUSTRATED, JOE ROBBINS, HERB
SCHARFMAN/SPORTS IMAGERY, RICK STEWART,
DAMIAN STROHMEYER/SPORTS ILLUSTRATED, AL
TIELEMANS/SPORTS ILLUSTRATED, TONY TOMSIC,
JARED WICKERHAM, LOU WITT/NFL), NEWSCOM
(ANTHONY NESMITH/CAL SPORT MEDIA)

LIBRARY OF CONGRESS CATALOGING-IN-PUBLICATION DATA
WHITING, JIM.
THE STORY OF THE NEW ENGLAND PATRIOTS / BY JIM WHITING.
P. CM. — (NFL TODAY)
INCLUDES INDEX.
SUMMARY: THE HISTORY OF THE NATIONAL FOOTBALL LEAGUE'S
NEW ENGLAND PATRIOTS, SURVEYING THE FRANCHISE'S BIGGEST
STARS AND MOST MEMORABLE MOMENTS FROM ITS INAUGURAL
SEASON IN 1960 TO TODAY.
ISBN 978-1-60818-310-4
1. NEW ENGLAND PATRIOTS (FOOTBALL TEAM)—HISTORY—
JUVENILE LITERATURE. I. TITLE.

GV956.N36W45 2013
796.332'640974461—DC23   2012031652

FIRST EDITION
9 8 7 6 5 4 3 2 1

COVER: LINEBACKER JEROD MAYO
PAGE 2: TIGHT END ROB GRONKOWSKI
PAGES 4–5: NEW ENGLAND PATRIOTS IN SUPER BOWL XLII
PAGE 6: GUARD JOHN HANNAH

TABLE OF CONTENTS

BOSTON, MASSACHUSETTS, IS THE LARGEST CITY IN NEW ENGLAND

The Team That Almost Wasn't

f George Washington is the father of America, then Boston, Massachusetts, might be called the country's cradle. Long a thorn in the side of the British monarchy, Boston earned more royal wrath for the "Boston Tea Party," in which a group of men posing as American Indians tossed dozens of crates of tea into Boston Harbor as a protest against British rule. The resulting crackdown only served to make Boston residents seethe even more. So it wasn't surprising that the "shot heard round the world"—the opening salvo of an eight-year struggle for independence—occurred in Lexington, a few miles away. Many iconic figures of the American Revolution, from Paul Revere to John Hancock, called the Boston area home. They had their work cut out for them, as a relative handful of patriots stood opposite the massive military forces of the British Empire. Frequently, the uprising teetered on the edge of collapse.

Gino Cappelletti

KICKER, WIDE RECEIVER / PATRIOTS SEASONS: 1960–70 / HEIGHT: 6 FEET / WEIGHT: 190 POUNDS

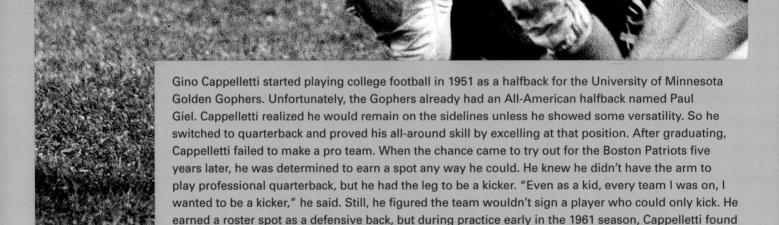

Gino Cappelletti started playing college football in 1951 as a halfback for the University of Minnesota Golden Gophers. Unfortunately, the Gophers already had an All-American halfback named Paul Giel. Cappelletti realized he would remain on the sidelines unless he showed some versatility. So he switched to quarterback and proved his all-around skill by excelling at that position. After graduating, Cappelletti failed to make a pro team. When the chance came to try out for the Boston Patriots five years later, he was determined to earn a spot any way he could. He knew he didn't have the arm to play professional quarterback, but he had the leg to be a kicker. "Even as a kid, every team I was on, I wanted to be a kicker," he said. Still, he figured the team wouldn't sign a player who could only kick. He earned a roster spot as a defensive back, but during practice early in the 1961 season, Cappelletti found himself filling in at wide receiver. He caught a pass and never went back to defense. He played receiver and kicker his entire career, amassing an astounding 1,130 points.

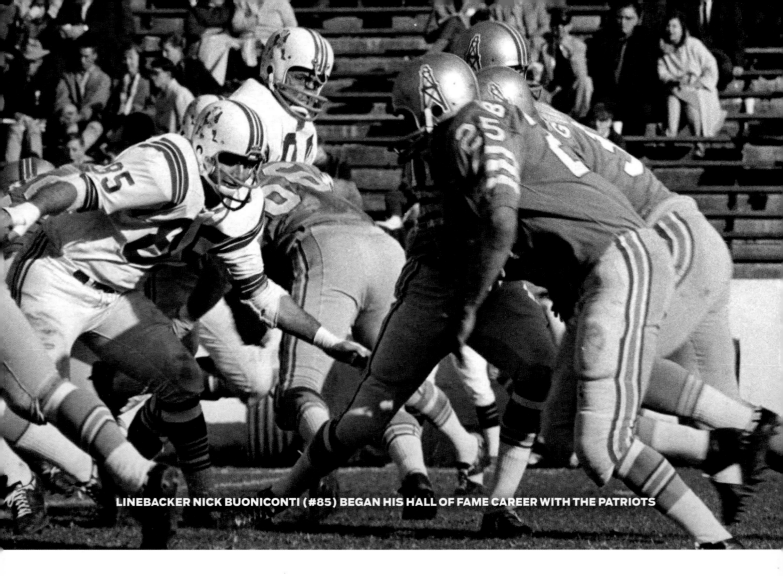

LINEBACKER NICK BUONICONTI (#85) BEGAN HIS HALL OF FAME CAREER WITH THE PATRIOTS

The New England Patriots could also be called "The Team That Almost Wasn't." Founding owner Billy Sullivan had little money and no home stadium in 1959 when he applied to join the upstart American Football League (AFL), a rival to the established National Football League (NFL). Sullivan did have a gift for persuasion, however, and the AFL needed an eighth team. As New England's premier city, Boston remained the most populous city (and largest television market) in the United States without a professional football team at that time.

After Lou Saban was hired as the Boston Patriots' first head coach, more than 350 players tried out for the team. Ed "Butch" Songin won the quarterback job. Although he was 36 years old and had been out of professional football for 6 years, he would surprise all doubters by passing for more than 2,400 yards in 1960. Another early standout was Gino Cappelletti, who played touch football to keep his skills sharp. He would make himself indispensable in Boston as a kicker and wide receiver.

During the 1960s, the Patriots played home games at Boston University Field, Boston College Alumni

"Guys would be bouncing off of him."

GINO CAPPELLETTI ON JIM NANCE

Field, Harvard Stadium, the Boston Red Sox's Fenway Park, and even Legion Field in Birmingham, Alabama. They finished a lowly 5–9 in 1960, and after the 1961 season started 2–3, assistant coach Mike Holovak replaced Saban. Vito "Babe" Parilli, a former backup with the Oakland Raiders, took over as quarterback. The team turned the season around to finish 9–4–1, placing second in the AFL's Eastern Division.

The Patriots built a strong defense around the likes of linebacker Nick Buoniconti, end Bob Dee, and tackle Jim Lee "Earthquake" Hunt. Buoniconti was the inspirational leader. Although many skeptics thought he was too small to play professional football, Buoniconti used his speed and smarts to become one of the greatest linebackers in football history.

The "Pats" held steady at 9–4–1 and second place in 1962 but dropped to 7–6–1 in 1963. Surprisingly, this record earned them their first postseason appearance, as the Patriots tied their divisional rival, the Buffalo Bills. Boston defeated Buffalo in a playoff game but was whipped 51–10 by the San Diego Chargers in the AFL Championship Game.

The Patriots placed second again in 1966, then finished with a losing record every season for the rest of the decade. Despite these lackluster results, players such as bulldozing fullback Jim Nance kept things exciting in Boston. "Guys would be bouncing off of him," Cappelletti recalled. Behind an offensive line anchored by 7-time All-Pro center Jon Morris, Nance piled up 5,323 career yards with the Patriots.

In 1970, the Patriots faced new challenges as the AFL merged with the NFL. The team still had no permanent home stadium, and its vagabond ways would not fly in the NFL. After various Boston stadium

One-Week Heroes

Although the Boston Patriots' 1963 season was far from glorious, it offered the team its first taste of championship football. The Patriots opened the season a mere 2–3, and at the season's end, they were annihilated 51–10 by the San Diego Chargers in the AFL Championship Game. But along the way, Boston won some key battles and captured the first playoff victory in team history. The unscheduled playoff was declared when Boston and the Buffalo Bills finished the season tied at 7–6–1. The two teams met in Buffalo in bitterly cold conditions on a slick, snow-covered field. Despite the weather, the Patriots attacked by air with long bombs and soaring kicks. Quarterback Vito Parilli hit running back Larry Garron with a 59-yard touchdown pass in the first quarter. In the third, he lofted a 51-yard completion to receiver Gino Cappelletti, which set up a 17-yard touchdown strike to Garron. As kicker, Cappelletti also chipped in four field goals and two extra points in the 26–8 Boston victory. For one week—until the unfortunate San Diego game—the Patriots were heroes.

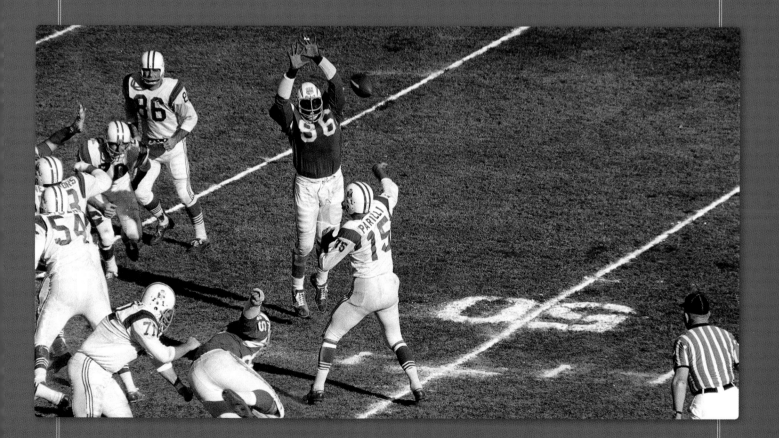

VITO "BABE" PARILLI QUARTERBACKED THE PATS TO THEIR FIRST PLAYOFF VICTORY

proposals failed, a plan to build in nearby Foxborough succeeded, and construction of Schaefer Stadium began in 1970. The Patriots played to a dismal 2–12 record that year but improved to 6–8 in 1971, including an upset victory over the Raiders in Schaefer Stadium's inaugural game.

Because it was not based in Boston anymore, the team was renamed the New England Patriots. Rookie quarterback Jim Plunkett tossed 19 touchdown passes in 1971 and won NFL Rookie of the Year honors. But neither Plunkett nor the new stadium turned the Patriots into a winning franchise. In 1973, Chuck Fairbanks, who had coached at the University of Oklahoma, was brought in.

John Hannah

GUARD / PATRIOTS SEASONS: 1973–85 / HEIGHT: 6-FOOT-2 / WEIGHT: 265 POUNDS

Many people believe that John "Hog" Hannah was the greatest offensive lineman in the history of the NFL. A fierce competitor who hated losing, Hannah exploded off the line of scrimmage like a cannonball, and his ferocious blocks could change a game. "He'd be responsible for blocking a linebacker on a certain play, and before you knew it, the linebacker would be down, and without slowing down, John would be out ahead taking out a cornerback," said Patriots quarterback Steve Grogan. "He would get two or three guys on those sweeps like no one I've ever seen." Hannah worked hard to succeed and seemed to underestimate his own abilities. "Contrary to what people say, I'm not a natural athlete," he said. "I have some gifts, but I can't just go out there and do it. I've got to think about what I do, because if I don't practice well, I won't play well." Hannah was legendary for practicing at full-steam all the time, and it showed on the field. In 1991, he was inducted into the Pro Football Hall of Fame.

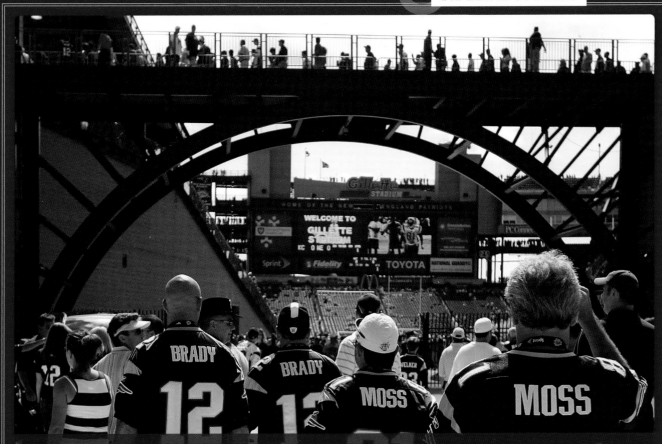

Sweet Home . . . Alabama

For several years in the 1960s, the Patriots called Fenway Park their primary home. The problem was that the Red Sox had first claim to the venue through early October, so the team often played four or five games on the road to start the season—hardly conducive to long-term success. Discouraged by dismal fan support and seeking a more permanent site for home games, owner Billy Sullivan decided to shop the team. So he scheduled a mid-September "home" game against the New York Jets at Legion Field in Birmingham, Alabama, more than 1,000 miles from Boston. At that time, the University of Alabama, with coach Paul "Bear" Bryant, had one of the country's dominant college programs, and Legion Field was dubbed the "Football Capital of the South." Some Birmingham civic leaders wanted to add a pro team to the city's football mix. Nearly 30,000 fans attended—more than twice the usual Boston-area turnout—but the stadium was still only about one-third full. Sullivan apparently decided that wasn't enough, and the Pats stayed put. With ex-Alabama standout Joe Namath quarterbacking the Jets, most fans rooted for the "visitors," and the Patriots dropped a 47–31 decision.

FOXBOROUGH'S GILLETTE STADIUM IS THE PATRIOTS' CURRENT HOME

The First Super Bowl Charge

Fairbanks's first move was to draft offensive lineman John "Hog" Hannah to give Plunkett better pass protection. Hannah also blocked for running back Sam "Bam" Cunningham, who would become New England's all-time leading rusher. Cunningham was famed for his ability to leap over men piled at the line of scrimmage in short-yardage situations. Although he only once topped 1,000 yards in a year during his 9 Patriots seasons, he averaged a stellar 3.9 yards per carry on 1,385 tries.

Although the talent level was rising, the Patriots never really jelled with Plunkett under center. His best effort produced a middling 7–7 record in 1974. When Plunkett was injured in 1975, rookie Steve Grogan took over. That season turned out even worse at 3–11, but Grogan showed he could handle pressure. Plunkett was traded,

ANDY JOHNSON (LEFT) AND SAM CUNNINGHAM FORMED A DYNAMIC DUO

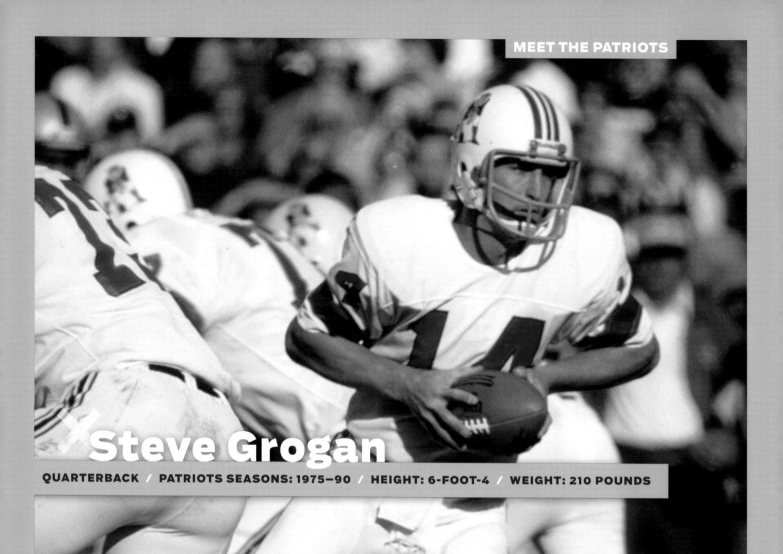

Steve Grogan

QUARTERBACK / PATRIOTS SEASONS: 1975–90 / HEIGHT: 6-FOOT-4 / WEIGHT: 210 POUNDS

Steve Grogan was a tough quarterback. During his career, he endured knee surgeries, elbow surgery, neck surgery, broken bones, separated shoulders, damaged ligaments, and several concussions. But if it was physically possible, he played. Grogan loved the rough-and-tumble game. Patriots center Bill Lenkaitis said this was never more obvious than when Grogan threw an interception. "Most quarterbacks try to hide," he said. "Grogan ran down and tried to knock the guy's head off." But Grogan wasn't all brawn and guts. He also had serious skill. He passed with precision for nearly 27,000 career yards, often tossing long bombs to his speedy receiving corps. The lanky field general also kept opposing defenses off balance with his scrambling and running ability. In 1976, he rushed for 12 touchdowns, which set an NFL single-season record for quarterbacks. Grogan's hard-nosed style of play often landed him at the doctor's office, but it also earned his teammates' respect. As Hall of Fame offensive lineman John Hannah said, "He was the kind of guy you wanted to protect, the kind of guy you wanted to play for."

"Grogan...tried to knock the guy's head off."

PATRIOTS CENTER BILL LENKAITIS

while Grogan led the 1976 Patriots to an 11–3 season and a playoff berth.

Wide receiver Darryl Stingley and tight end Russ Francis emerged as Grogan's favorite targets. Stingley was acrobatic and fearless in running routes across the dangerous middle part of the field, while the 6-foot-6 and 240-pound Francis possessed uncommon speed and soft hands for a player his size. On defense, cornerback Mike Haynes grabbed 8 interceptions and zigzagged his way to more than 600 yards returning punts in 1976. These players made New England a force to be reckoned with. "The '76 team was the best I ever played on," Hannah said. Unfortunately, that talented Patriots club met an abrupt end in the playoffs. New England had bested Oakland during the regular season, but the Raiders pulled out a 24–21 victory when quarterback Ken Stabler ran for a touchdown with 10 seconds remaining.

After a 9–5 season in 1977, New England came back strong in 1978, winning the American Football Conference (AFC) East Division and reaching the playoffs again. But it was a bittersweet year that ended badly and started even worse. Going for a catch in a preseason game against Oakland, Stingley took a vicious hit that left him paralyzed. The team rallied in the face of Stingley's sad and unexpected exit, earning 11 wins. It could not, however, rally in the postseason. Foxborough's first-ever playoff game saw the Patriots pummeled by the Houston Oilers, 31–14.

Perhaps more than any other sport, football is a coach's game, with outcomes decided by strategy, game-time decisions, and the ability to manage and motivate players. After the departure of Chuck Fairbanks in 1978, the Patriots' success diminished according to the ability of their coaches.

Coach Ron Erhardt was too easygoing. His teams started strong but finished poorly, dropping five of their last eight games in 1979, five of their last nine in 1980, and their last nine en route to a 2–14 record in 1981. Erhardt failed to control his players, while his successor, Ron Meyer, tried too hard to control them. Meyer made unnecessary rules, such as no sitting on helmets during practice and no eating popsicles at training

A Kick in the Snow

On a freezing December afternoon in 1982, the Patriots met the Miami Dolphins on an ice- and snow-covered Schaefer Stadium field. Linemen had little traction for blocking. Running backs slipped and slid. Kickers found no footing to launch their kicks. In the second quarter, Patriots kicker John Smith missed an 18-yard field goal. "My leg went flying up in the air, and I drove the ball right into John Hannah's butt," he said. Dolphins kicker Uwe Von Schamann muffed a 45-yarder—also into a lineman's backside. The game remained scoreless until New England gained a final chance with under five minutes remaining. Patriots coach Ron Meyer called a play for Mark Henderson, driver of the tractor and snow sweeper used to clear the yard lines. "We had called timeout so John Smith could clear a patch for himself. Then I saw the sweeper and just went down and told him to sweep," Meyer said. "Great coaching genius, I guess." Henderson cleared a spot for Smith, who knocked one through the uprights for a 3–0 New England victory.

SNOWPLOW DRIVER MARK HENDERSON CLEARED A SPOT FOR A GAME-WINNING KICK

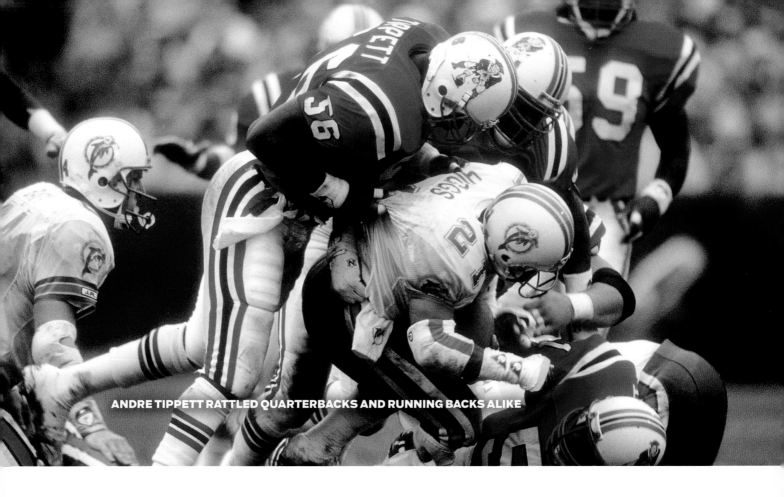

ANDRE TIPPETT RATTLED QUARTERBACKS AND RUNNING BACKS ALIKE

camp. While he had better results than Erhardt—a 5–4 record in a strike-shortened 1982 season and an 8–8 mark in 1983—his players rebelled against him, and he was fired halfway through his third season.

Former Patriots assistant coach Raymond Berry had been away from football for two and a half years when the team offered him the head coaching job in 1984. A kind man who was well liked, Berry encouraged his team with a respectful coaching style. "He treated everyone like a man," Patriots linebacker Steve Nelson said. "He assumed we had the same goals he had—to win every game."

Nelson, who spent his entire 14-year NFL career with New England, met opposing ballcarriers like a brick wall, collecting more than 100 tackles in 9 different seasons. If Nelson was a wall, Andre Tippett was a hurricane. One of a new breed of outside linebackers who emerged during the 1980s, Tippett could chase down smaller running backs and was just as effective at storming the passer. Tippett recorded 16.5 sacks in 1985 and would eventually set the Patriots' career mark of 100. Opposing offenses who tried to throw over the Patriots' ferocious linebackers had to contend with another formidable defender in star defensive back Raymond Clayborn.

The Patriots got off to a 2–3 start in 1985 but then rattled off six straight wins after Steve Grogan took over for an injured Tony Eason at quarterback. When Grogan was injured late in the season, Eason

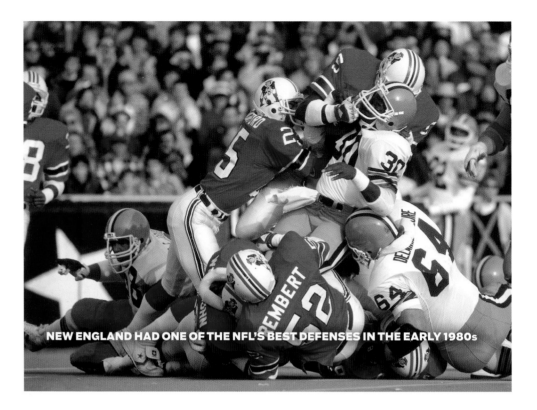

NEW ENGLAND HAD ONE OF THE NFL'S BEST DEFENSES IN THE EARLY 1980s

returned and won three of four games to lead New England into the playoffs with an 11–5 record. Speedy wide receiver Stanley Morgan was a favorite target of both passers. The Patriots' true offensive strength, however, was their dominant running game, which was led by halfback Craig James and piled up more than 2,300 yards. Veteran guard John Hannah played heroically through numerous injuries to anchor the offensive line in his final season.

In the playoffs, New England won three road games, including a comeback from 17–7 down against the Los Angeles Raiders and a 31–14 rout of the Miami Dolphins in the AFC Championship Game. In the Super Bowl, however, New England was flattened by the mighty Chicago Bears, 46–10. To the puzzlement of many fans and even players, the Patriots came out passing despite having relied on their running game all year. "Well, the one thing the Bears can't say today is they stopped our running game," said James. "Because we didn't run it."

New England went 11–5 again in 1986 but lost to the Denver Broncos in the first round of the playoffs. The team fell to 5–11 by 1989, Berry's last year, and hit rock bottom at 1–15 the next year under new coach Rod Rust.

Squish the Fish

When the Patriots faced off against the Miami Dolphins in the 1985 AFC Championship Game, they had something to prove. They had not won a game in Miami's Orange Bowl stadium in 19 years. But fresh off two road playoff wins, New England's players seemed unconcerned with the past and took advantage of soggy field conditions with a punishing ground game. "[The coaches] came to the offensive line and said, 'It's on you,'" said Patriots center Pete Brock. "'Oh, boy,' we thought, 'we're gonna run the ball in the mud.' And we did." The Patriots amassed 255 yards on 59 carries, with halfback Craig James rushing for 105 yards behind the muddy offensive line. The Patriots also recovered four Miami fumbles en route to a 31–14 victory. "It was 'Squish the Fish,'" said Patriots linebacker Andre Tippett. "We had never won down there, but we just walked into the Orange Bowl, and we weren't going to be denied." With the team's first victory in the Orange Bowl, New England also reached its first Super Bowl.

ROBERT WEATHERS SCORED A TOUCHDOWN IN THE 1985 AFC CHAMPIONSHIP GAME

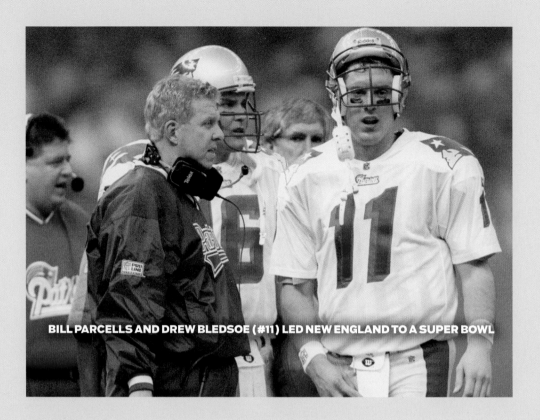

BILL PARCELLS AND DREW BLEDSOE (#11) LED NEW ENGLAND TO A SUPER BOWL

From Parcells to Belichick

After their abysmal 1990 season, the Patriots needed dramatic changes. They got them in the form of new ownership in 1992 and a new coach and new look in 1993. Out was the team's old-fashioned, colonial-garbed hiking patriot logo, and in was a modern, grim-faced patriot image. Also in was coach Bill Parcells, who had won two Super Bowls at the helm of the New York Giants. When team ownership changed hands yet again in 1994, local businessman Robert Kraft provided the leadership necessary to build a championship team.

The new-look Patriots selected quarterback Drew Bledsoe with the first overall pick of the 1993 NFL Draft. In his second season, Bledsoe led New England to a seven-game winning streak and its first playoff appearance since 1986. But the 10–6 Patriots lost to the Cleveland Browns in a muddy first-round game in Cleveland Stadium, with Bledsoe throwing three interceptions. "Right now," Bledsoe said, "It feels like a disaster,

QUARTERBACK DREW BLEDSOE SPENT NINE SEASONS WITH THE PATRIOTS

✗ Stanley Morgan

WIDE RECEIVER / PATRIOTS SEASONS: 1977–89 / HEIGHT: 5-FOOT-11 / WEIGHT: 181 POUNDS

Stanley Morgan, wrote one reporter, was a "touchdown waiting to happen." His quickness and straight-ahead speed allowed him to average 19.4 yards per reception in an era when defensive backs were permitted to clobber receivers all the way down the field. Morgan had a knack for keeping defenders on their heels and then leaving them in the dust. "When he was running those posts, those free safeties had to really get on their horse and get back there because he'd get on top of you in a hurry," Patriots coach Bill Belichick said. Once he caught the ball, Morgan was off to the races, with the end zone as the finish line. He was one of the game's speeding bullets, often gone before defenders could get a hand on him. "I remember Stanley going deep on those go-routes with nobody out there to catch him," said Patriots linebacker Andre Tippett. "Whenever you saw him open like that, you knew it was a touchdown." In 1989, Morgan caught his 67th Patriots touchdown reception, which remains the most in team history.

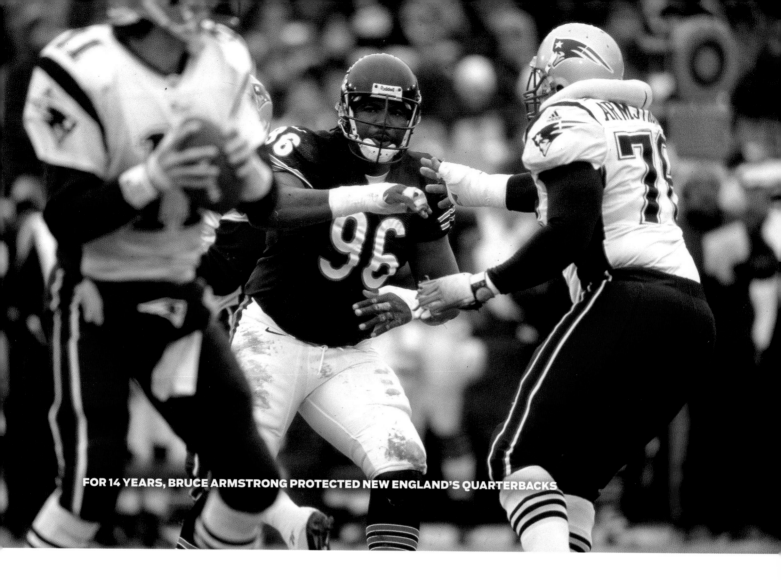

FOR 14 YEARS, BRUCE ARMSTRONG PROTECTED NEW ENGLAND'S QUARTERBACKS

because we just lost. But I guess if you look at it with some perspective, it was a good season."

In 1995, Bledsoe injured his shoulder, and New England dipped to 6–10. One bright spot was rookie running back Curtis Martin, who cut and slashed his way to 1,487 yards and 14 touchdowns. Martin, Bledsoe, and their teammates rebounded big time in 1996. The offensive line, anchored by tackle Bruce Armstrong, kept Bledsoe healthy. Wide receiver Terry Glenn proved a long-bomb threat, setting an NFL rookie receiving record with 90 catches. Adding more muscle to the Patriots' air attack was Ben Coates, a big, powerful, and fast tight end. "We have as many weapons as probably anybody in the league right now," Bledsoe said.

Loaded with talent, the 1996 Patriots went 11–5 and made the playoffs. They trounced the Pittsburgh Steelers in a foggy game in Foxborough and dispatched the Jacksonville Jaguars in a bitterly cold AFC Championship Game the following Sunday. Led by defensive end Willie McGinest, linebacker Chris Slade, and safety Lawyer Milloy, the Patriots' dominating defense held their opponents to nine points and no touchdowns in the two games.

I n Super Bowl XXXI versus the Green Bay Packers, the Patriots came back from a 10–0 deficit in the first quarter to take a 14–10 lead and climbed to within striking distance at 27–21 after being down 27–14 at halftime. In the end, though, Green Bay's strong offense and stellar kick-return play proved to be more than New England could overcome in a 35–21 loss.

Coach Parcells left the team after the defeat, and the Pats steadily sank. In 1997, they won one game fewer than in 1996 and lost in the second round of the playoffs. In 1998, they won one game fewer than in 1997 and lost in the first round of the playoffs. And in 1999, they won one game fewer than in 1998, leaving them at 8–8 and out of the playoffs. Once more, it was time for a change.

When Bill Belichick led New England to a 5–11 record in 2000, his first season as

DAVE MEGGETT WAS THE PATRIOTS' TOP KICK RETURNER IN SUPER BOWL XXXI

A Kick in the Snow, Part 2

The snow was swirling, the wind was whipping, and the game was on the line. But like the New England winter itself, Patriots kicker Adam Vinatieri had ice in his veins. It was January 19, 2002, and the Patriots trailed the Oakland Raiders 10–13 in an AFC playoff matchup. With 27 seconds left in the game, 4 inches of snow on the ground, and 45 yards between him and the goalposts, Vinatieri stepped onto the field. He knew he had to make the kick or the season was over. Raiders coach Jon Gruden called a timeout, trying to "ice" the kicker by giving him time to grow nervous. "I'm not sure 'icing the kicker' actually works," Vinatieri said. "I think having a little extra time to clear the footing helps the situation." Despite Gruden's ploy, the snowy conditions, and the nerve-racking circumstances, Vinatieri knocked a low, warbling kick through the uprights. "I don't know if I've ever kicked in conditions worse than that," Vinatieri said. "It's probably the biggest kick I've ever had." For good measure, Vinatieri also booted a 23-yard game-winner in overtime.

ADAM VINATIERI MADE MANY CLUTCH FIELD GOALS FOR THE PATRIOTS

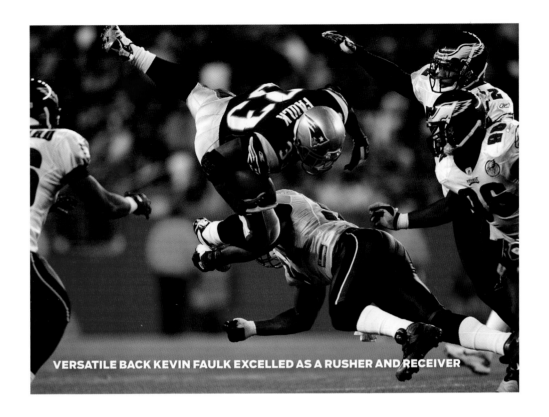

VERSATILE BACK KEVIN FAULK EXCELLED AS A RUSHER AND RECEIVER

the Patriots' new head coach, many fans thought his hiring had been a mistake. Although he had proven himself a brilliant defensive coordinator, engineering the dominating Giants defense of the 1980s, he had been unsuccessful in five years as the Cleveland Browns' head coach. But Belichick, along with owner Robert Kraft, had a plan to build a winner: assemble a group of team players that could achieve more than the sum of its stars.

A key piece of this plan fell into place in the second game of the 2001 season, when second-year quarterback Tom Brady stepped in for an injured Bledsoe. The Patriots lost that game, and for the next eight contests, Brady's play was spotty. But Belichick saw something in Brady. It wasn't pure physical ability. There were intangible skills. Brady was a natural leader.

Belichick stuck with Brady, even after Bledsoe recovered, and the coach's faith in the young quarterback paid off. In the 11th game of the season, a victory over the New Orleans Saints, New England jelled as a unit. It didn't lose another game the rest of the year, including Super Bowl XXXVI, in which the Patriots shocked the highflying and heavily favored St. Louis Rams, 20–17, on a last-second field goal by kicker Adam Vinatieri. "You can't beat a team like the Rams with individuals," Milloy said. "It takes a team. That's what you saw today."

The championship-clinching upset was a true team effort. While Brady won the game's Most Valuable Player (MVP) award, Vinatieri could also have taken that prize. Or it could have gone to linebacker Tedy Bruschi or other players on the Patriots defense, which held the Rams to 17 points—14 below their season average.

ALL-PRO RICHARD SEYMOUR BOLSTERED THE PATRIOTS' DEFENSIVE LINE

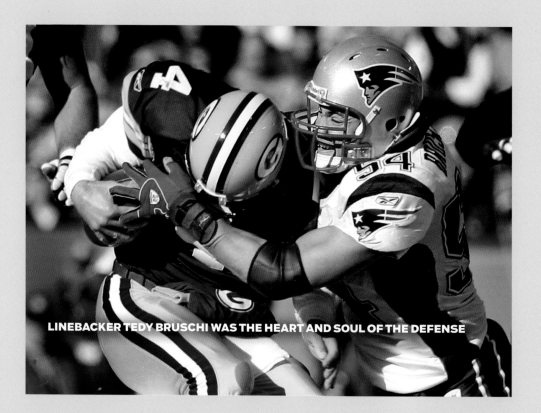

LINEBACKER TEDY BRUSCHI WAS THE HEART AND SOUL OF THE DEFENSE

Patriots Pride

Teamwork and smart play kept the Patriots rolling. In 2003, New England went 14–2 to win the AFC East. In the playoffs, the Patriots first faced a tough Tennessee Titans squad and prevailed, 17–14. In the AFC Championship Game, New England battled the Indianapolis Colts. The Patriots' physical defense stifled the Colts' potent offense, creating five turnovers in a 24–14 victory. Super Bowl XXXVIII, between the Patriots and the Carolina Panthers, again came down to the wire. In the fourth quarter, with the score tied 29–29, Brady led his team down the field. Vinatieri sealed the victory with a 41-yard field goal with four seconds remaining.

The next year, the Patriots again went 14–2. They crushed the Colts 20–3 in the playoffs behind running back Corey Dillon's 144 rushing yards, then triumphed over the Steelers in a 41–27 AFC Championship Game slugfest. In a Super Bowl matchup against the Philadelphia Eagles, wide receiver Deion Branch tied a Super Bowl record by grabbing 11 receptions, and the Patriots' defense held off a late Eagles charge to

ADAM VINATIERI'S LAST-SECOND KICK WON SUPER BOWL XXXVIII

Tom Brady

QUARTERBACK / PATRIOTS SEASONS: 2000–PRESENT / HEIGHT: 6-FOOT-4 / WEIGHT: 225 POUNDS

In 2002, after Tom Brady's first season as the Patriots' starting quarterback, the team won its first Super Bowl. By 2005, New England had won two more. One could argue that Brady owed his success to his hard work in practice, his preparation, and his determination to always improve—and all of these things would be true. But at the heart of it, Brady won because he played his best when it counted the most. "Nerves come from not knowing what to do," he explained. "If you're confident going out there that you know what you're going to do ... that's when you feel best." Not particularly fast or strong-armed, Brady overcame any physical shortcomings with his poise and intelligence. "He can see the defense, what they're doing, and can sort it out in a hurry," said Patriots coach Bill Belichick. "You'll never see him panic." While Brady earned a reputation as one of the greatest quarterbacks of all time, he also became something of a style icon off the field. In 2007, *Esquire* magazine called him the "best dressed man in the world," and in 2009, he married fashion supermodel Gisele Bündchen.

preserve a 24–21 victory.

The Patriots came down to earth with playoff losses in 2005 and 2006. Then, in 2007, New England came within one game of football immortality. After adding star receivers Randy Moss and Wes Welker through trades, the Patriots went undefeated in the regular season, setting a new NFL scoring record with 589 points. After beating the Jaguars and San Diego Chargers in the playoffs, New England reached its fourth Super Bowl in seven years and was poised to become the first team in NFL history to go 19–0.

The heavily favored Patriots met the Giants in Super Bowl XLII and seemed to have the game in hand when they took a 14–10 lead with under three minutes remaining. But the Giants mounted an

NEW ENGLAND HAS BEEN TO SEVEN SUPER BOWLS AND WON THREE TITLES

83-yard drive, scoring a touchdown with 35 seconds left to upset the Patriots 17–14. "I think we all feel the same way," Belichick said. "I wish we could have done one thing a little better, and it might have changed it. But we didn't."

In 2008, New England's title hopes seemed to go up in smoke in the very first game, when Brady was lost for the year with a knee injury. Although backup quarterback Matt Cassel played well, the Patriots just missed the playoffs. Brady returned in 2009 and earned Comeback Player of the Year honors as the Pats returned to the postseason. The home fans were left stunned, though, as Baltimore sped to a 24–0 first-quarter lead in a first-round matchup and coasted to a 33–14 triumph. The following year, Brady had one of his finest seasons, completing 335 passes and earning the league's MVP award as the team earned the top seed in the AFC with a 14–2 mark. But the New York Jets eliminated the Patriots in the playoffs, 28–21.

Despite those setbacks, the Patriots seemed to have a knack for continually turning up enough talent to remain postseason contenders. In 2010, running back BenJarvus Green-Ellis gave the team its first 1,000-yard rusher in 6 years. That same year, New England shored up its tight end position by drafting Rob Gronkowski, who had a breakout season in 2011, setting several NFL records for tight ends. New England fans also gave Gronkowski and another tight end a nickname: the "Boston TE Party," a nod to the famous 1773 event.

Spreading the Wealth

A game in which quarterback Tom Brady threw for just 153 yards and the Patriots were outgained overall 400 yards to 265 might sound like bad news for New England. Yet the Patriots romped over the Miami Dolphins by a score of 41–14 on October 4, 2010. With New England scoring just a pair of field goals in the first half and trailing 7–6 in the *Monday Night Football* matchup, receiver Brandon Tate returned the second-half kickoff 103 yards for a touchdown. Two minutes later, running back BenJarvus Green-Ellis scored on a 12-yard run. Still in the third quarter, Brady answered a Dolphins touchdown with an 11-yard scoring toss to running back Danny Woodhead. In the final period, safety Patrick Chung blocked a Miami field goal attempt, and cornerback Kyle Arrington scooped up the loose ball and scampered 35 yards for a score. Chung closed out the scoring when he intercepted a pass by Dolphins quarterback Chad Henne and went 51 yards the other way. The Patriots thereby became the first team in NFL history to score a rushing touchdown, a receiving touchdown, a kickoff return touchdown, a blocked field-goal touchdown, and an interception return touchdown in the same game.

TOM BRADY WON HIS SECOND NFL MVP AWARD IN 2010

HAVING A STRONG DEFENSE HAS BEEN CRITICAL TO NEW ENGLAND'S SUCCESS

43

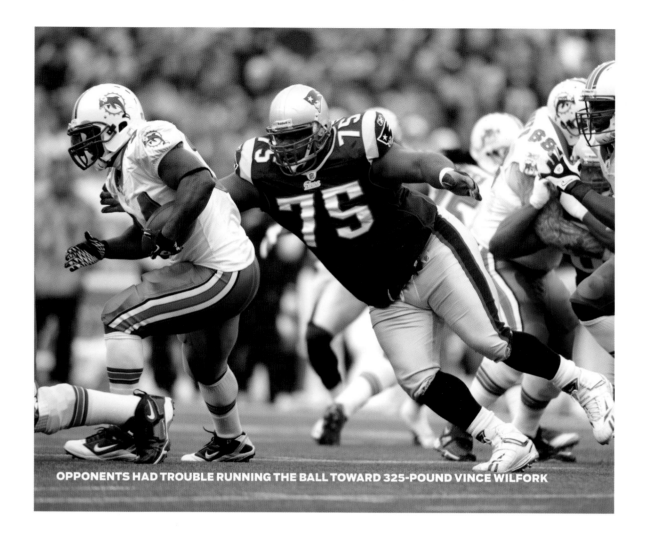

OPPONENTS HAD TROUBLE RUNNING THE BALL TOWARD 325-POUND VINCE WILFORK

Gronkowski was particularly beastly in 2011, establishing several NFL records for tight ends: most touchdown receptions (17), most overall touchdowns (18), and most receiving yards (1,327). Former New England quarterback Drew Bledsoe summed up the matchup problems the 6-foot-6 and 265-pound "Gronk" created. "It's kind of like having [basketball star] LeBron James playing tight end for you," he said. "He's too big for the slow guys and too fast for the small guys."

The Boston TE Party played a key role as New England went 13–3 in 2011. In the playoffs, the Patriots dominated Denver 45–10 and squeaked past Baltimore 23–20 to gain entry to Super Bowl XLVI. Unfortunately, Gronkowski had suffered a severe ankle sprain in the AFC title game, leaving Brady without one of his favorite targets on Super Bowl Sunday. In that game, the Giants once again foiled the Patriots, claiming the Lombardi Trophy by pulling out a closely fought, 21–17 victory.

Bill Belichick

COACH / PATRIOTS SEASONS: 2000–PRESENT

Bill Belichick learned his *X*s and *O*s at an early age from his father Steve, a longtime assistant coach at the U.S. Naval Academy. Belichick began his NFL coaching career with the Baltimore Colts in 1975 at age 22, getting $25 a week. After a five-year stint as Cleveland's head coach in the early 1990s, Belichick was hired in New England in 2000 and went 5–11 his first season. He restocked the team with players such as linebacker Mike Vrabel, a bust in Pittsburgh. "I didn't think anyone would find a way to use me," Vrabel said. "But I was amazed how much Bill knew about me.... In situational football, which is basically what the NFL is today, he's got to be the best mind out there." It never seemed to matter if key Patriots players were out of the lineup, what the media was talking about, or what the weather was going to be—Belichick stayed focused on the game. "You just try to take the situation at hand and do the best you can with it," he said. Belichick's "best" produced 3 Super Bowl wins—and 5 appearances—in an 11-year span.

WES WELKER CAUGHT MORE THAN 100 PASSES IN 5 DIFFERENT SEASONS

DEFENSIVE END CHANDLER JONES (#95) AND LINEBACKER DONT'A HIGHTOWER

The 2012 season began in humdrum fashion, but then New England caught fire, winning 9 of its final 10 games and scoring 557 points—the third-best mark in NFL history. The Pats' 12–4 record gave them the AFC East title for the fourth year in a row and earned a first-round bye in the playoffs. Brady then surpassed 49ers great Joe Montana as the winningest quarterback in postseason play with New England's 41–28 win over Houston in the divisional round of the playoffs. "I think I've just been fortunate to play on some great teams over the years," said Brady. "I never take it for granted."

Facing the tough Ravens defense the following week in the AFC Championship Game, the Patriots took a 13–7 halftime edge and seemed to have history on their side: During Brady's tenure, they had gone undefeated at home when leading at halftime. But Baltimore rewrote the history books by shutting out New England in the second half, leaving Pats fans bitterly disappointed.

The New England Patriots may have started slow, but since Belichick took over in 2000, they have stood on or near the top of the NFL more seasons than not. In that span, the team in red, white, and blue has racked up an impressive 151–57 regular-season record as of the end of the 2012 season and captured three Super Bowl victories while missing the playoffs just twice. As the Patriots continue to go to battle with a combination of crafty coaching, tight-knit team play, and New England's trademark tenacity, they might soon reign as football kings once again.